BATH

IN

50

BUILDINGS

PAT DARGAN

AMBERLEY

First published 2018

Amberley Publishing, The Hill, Stroud
Gloucestershire GL5 4EP

www.amberley-books.com

British Library Cataloguing in Publication Data.
A catalogue record for this book is available from the British Library.

ISBN 978 1 4456 5963 3 (print)
ISBN 978 1 4456 5964 0 (ebook)

Origination by Amberley Publishing.
Printed in Great Britain.

Contents

Introduction

The city of Bath lies mainly within a wide sweep of the River Avon in the county of Somerset and features a range of eighteenth- and nineteenth-century buildings that mark the city as one of the most elegant Georgian urban centres in the British Isles. The building fabric of the city is unique in Britain in that most of the buildings are built with an attractive honey-coloured Bath stone. The fifty buildings presented here have been chosen by the writer as best representing the most iconic examples of the city's domestic, commercial and religious architecture, and are presented in the historical sequence in which they were completed: the medieval, Georgian, Gothic Revival, and modern periods. The geographical area chosen for the presentation represents the historic Georgian centre of Bath, which is the area enclosed by the river between the Royal Crescent and Great Pulteney Street.

The origins of Bath lie in the Roman settlement of Aquae Sulis, which was established during the first century AD on the site of the thermal spring – the only one in the British Isles. Little is known about the form of the Roman town, as nothing survives of the settlement above ground level. Following the withdrawal of the Romans the settlement remained in use throughout the medieval period, and developed as a prosperous walled town. During this period the Benedictine abbey was established and the abbey church was built around 1499. Today the abbey church is the only surviving medieval building in Bath, as the rest of the town's medieval fabric was removed during the extensive developments of the city during the Georgian period of the eighteenth and nineteenth centuries. During this period the development of the city was underpinned by the availability of the thermal springs, the business acumen of Ralph Allen, the owner of the quarry that produced the Bath stone, the skill of John Wood, the architect who was largely responsible for the design of the characteristic squares, crescents and uniform streets of Georgian buildings, and the commitment of Richard Beau Nash, who guided the cultural and social aspects of the Enlightenment in Bath.

In contrast to the characteristic uniformity of the Georgian architecture, a number of Gothic Revival buildings were also completed in Bath in an attempt to recreate the Gothic and other architecture styles of earlier periods. During the twentieth century building activity in Bath was largely based on the use of neo-Georgian elements, so as to blend in with the overall concept of the Georgian city, and in 1987 UNESCO added the city of Bath to its World Heritage List.

Among the reasons for Bath's inclusion was the acknowledgement of the 'eighteenth century city as a masterpiece of human creative genius'. It was not really until the twenty-first century that an attempt was made to introduce new architectural concepts into Bath's historic area, when a number of significant examples, such as the New Royal Bath, were completed.

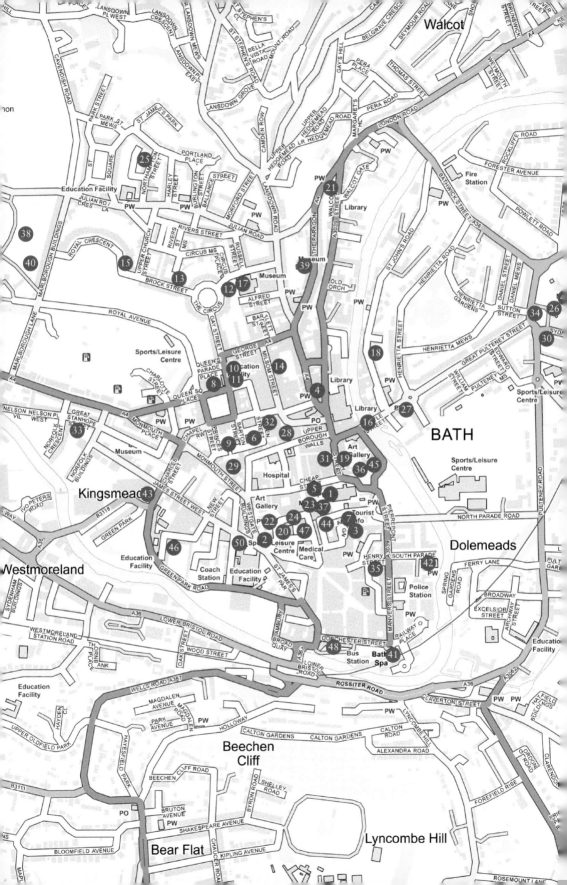

Key

The 50 Buildings

1. Bath Abbey, Abbey Church Yard

The Gothic Church of St Peter and St Paul, commonly known as Bath Abbey, dates from 1502, although the origins of the church date to the twelfth-century Benediction priory, but by the early sixteenth century the building had deteriorated and in 1502 the church was rebuilt on the foundations of an earlier structure. Following the Dissolution of the Monasteries, the church came into the possession of the Colthurst family, who gave it to the city to become the parish

The south elevation of Bath Abbey with the elaborate flying buttresses and Gothic windows of the nave, aisle and south transept.

A night image of the west elevation of Bath Abbey, opening onto Abbey Church Yard.

Bath Abbey nave with the arcade arches, clerestory windows, fan vaulting and east window.

church in 1572. Following this, the church was restored, particularly during the nineteenth century, when the fan vault, tracery and flying buttresses were inserted. The three-bay west elevation fronts onto the Abbey Church Yard and offers all the characteristic features of Gothic architecture: pointed doors and windows, elaborate tracery, gables, figure sculpture, and a pair of buttresses that mark the different roof heights of the nave and aisles. A curious feature of the buttresses is the ladders on which carved angelic figures rise and descend. The side elevations have a range of Gothic windows on both the lower and higher levels, as well as flying buttress. Internally the nave is separated from the side aisles by an arcade of arches. The arches are carried on piers faced with rounded shafts, the outer one of which rises to the roof level and spreads out to form spectacular fan vaulting. This extends along the full length of the church, while the east end of the nave culminates in a magnificent east window.

2. Abbey Church House, Westgate Buildings

Abbey Church House was built for Edward Clarke in 1550 and passed through several ownerships, including Dr Robert Baker, who acquired the house to provide lodgings for his patients adjacent to the hot baths. The building is illustrated in Joseph Gilmore's map of 1692, the only building in the map that survives from that period, except for Bath Abbey. The building was almost completely destroyed by bombing 1942 and was largely rebuilt in the 1950s. This includes the front elevation, which was completely rebuilt from pre-war records. The building is laid out in an L-shaped arrangement, with main elevation opening onto Westgate Buildings, and the side elevation fronting onto Hetling Court. The Westgate Buildings elevation is three storeys high over basement and three bays across the front, each with a front-facing roof gable. The elevation also has a range of mullion and transom windows on each floor. These are divided into individual panes by stone uprights and crosspieces, hence the name.

The Westgate Buildings elevation of Abbey Church House with its forward-facing roof gables and central doorway.

The bay windows of Abbey Church House with stone mullions and transoms.

The Hetling Court elevation is considerably longer. It is similarly arranged in six bays with upper-floor gables and mullioned windows, although the east end has been considerably altered and extended. A prominent element of the building is the elaborate chimney with three diagonal flues arranged in independent stacks. Although subjected to extensive rebuilding, Abbey Church House presents an accurate impression of the original building. Today the house is in private ownership with no access to the public.

3. No. 4 North Parade Passage (Sally Lunn's House)

No. 4 North Parade Passage can be dated to a lease made out to George Parker in 1622. Although it has suffered many alterations over time, parts of the medieval structure survive internally. The house stands in a narrow street amongst a terrace

Above: The narrow North Parade Passage is lined with differently sized houses from various historic periods.

Left: Bowed shopfront of Sally Lunn's House, No. 4 North Passage Parade.

Section of plasterwork of No. 4 North Passage Parade removed to expose medieval structural timbers.

of mixed houses and housed Ralph Allen's first Post Office of 1725. Today the building is four storeys high over basement level, although the basement level was once ground level before the street level was raised around 1750. Sally Lunn's Restaurant operates on the ground level with its side entrance door and a bowed bay window of around 1750. Overhead the first, second and third floors have paired sash windows on each level, a continuous drip mould that separates each floor level, and a forward facing roof gable. An interesting feature is a section of the internal plasterwork that has been removed to expose the medieval structural timbers. Apart from the restaurant the building is not accessible to the public.

4. The Saracen's Head Inn, Broad Street

The Saracen's Head is a pub and restaurant located on Broad Street, set between the Church of St Michael and St Paul and the Georgian streetscape. The choice of name is not unusual. It was commonly used in the naming of taverns and inns and is derived from the medieval heraldry symbol of a Saracen's head. The building is three storeys high with a forward-facing double gabled attic floor and a tiled roof visible from the street. The building may originally have been a pair. The date stone in one of the gables reads '1713'. The street elevation has plain corner

The Saracen's Head Inn, with its double gables and 1713 date stone, opens directly onto Broad Street.

quoins at both ends and a slightly projecting entrance porch at ground level, with an inserted Georgian-style shopfront to one side. On the other side of the porch is a single up-and-down sliding sash window. The first floor has four sash windows, each with moulded surrounds, while the top floor has a small sash window with hood mouldings located midpoint in each of the two gables. Curiously, each of the gables has a tall rectangular-shaped chimney stack directly over each of the windows. The building once held a shop and a library and Charles Dickens is reputed to have stayed here in 1835.

5. General Wade's House, Abbey Church Yard

General George Wade was initially commissioned as an officer into the Earl of Bath's regiment. He took part in a number of military campaigns during the seventeenth and eighteenth centuries in addition to undertaking security duties in Bath. The general's house, which was built around 1700, opens directly onto Abbey Church Yard. It was one of the earliest Georgian houses to have been built in Bath and it was inspired by the Palladian designs of Inigo Jones's houses in Covent Garden, London. The building is four storeys high with five flat fluted columns rising through the first and second floor and tall windows positioned

General Wade's House, with its Palladian and Regency elements, forms part of the mixed Abbey Church Yard terrace.

The nineteenth-century curved shopfront and side door of General Wade's House, with delicate Regency trimmings.

between each set of columns. These are standard up-and-down sliding sashes with multiple panes – a standard Georgian window format that occurs again and again throughout the development of Georgian Bath. Above the columns a deep moulded cornice stretches across the full width of the building, overhead, which the lines of the columns are continued to the underside of the moulded parapet, with square attic windows above. During the nineteenth century the ground floor level was converted to retail use and a Regency-style shopfront was inserted at ground level. This has a curved front, an elaborate fascia and a side door, all with delicate Regency trimmings. The house is now part of a mixed terrace, although the ground and first floors are in retail use with public access. There is no public access to the accommodation on the upper levels.

6. No. 5 Trim Street (General Wolfe's House)

Although referred to as 'General Wolfe's House', No. 5 Trim Street was the home of Wolfe's parents, where he stayed in 1759, before fighting and defeating the French in Quebec in the same year. The house, which was designed by the architect Thomas Greenway, dates from around 1720, and is positioned on the narrow street within a mixed terrace of two- and three-storey houses.

Above left: No. 5 Trim Street is integrated into the mixed Georgian terraced streetscape and has a range of standard Palladian elements including quoins, a central doorcase, fluted columns, curved pediments and a plain parapet.

Above right: The door of No. 5 Trim Street is framed with metal railings, flanking columns and curved pediment with a military-style memorial panel set beneath the pediment curve.

Curved pediment plaque to General Wolfe's house celebrates his military achievements.

The symmetrically arranged double storey over basement house is decidedly Palladian in style. This includes five standard sash-window bays across the front and plain metal railings that separate the house and basement area from the street. The building has plain quoins at both ends and the standard sash Georgian windows throughout have moulded surrounds. The entrance door is flanked on each side by flat fluted columns as well as a curved overhead pediment. These column and pediment elements are repeated on the second-floor window. At attic level, the small windows are almost hidden by the plain parapet. An interesting feature of the central doorway is the curved military plaque that sits in the pediment and celebrates the military career of the general. The house is now in office use with no access to the public.

7. Ralph Allen's House, North Passage Parade and York Street

Ralph Allen's house originally stood in North Passage Parade, although layout and position of the house is uncertain. What is certain is that Allen, the Bath stone quarry owner, added an extension to his house in 1727, although the relationship of the extension to the main house is uncertain. The design has been attributed to John Wood the Elder, but this is equally uncertain. Today, Allen's extension,

As it is in a private and restricted courtyard, access to view the Palladian elevation of Ralph Allen's House extension is limited. Despite this it remains one of the most elegant examples of Bath's Georgian heritage.

the only part of his house to survive, faces into a tiny enclosed courtyard that is accessible only from York Street. Despite this it represents a remarkably elegant piece of Bath's Georgian heritage. The elevation is tall and narrow and consists of a three-storey building, with a rusticated ground level, double-storey columns on the two upper floors and an elaborate triangular pediment.

The ground level has three sash windows with key stones, the central one set into a semicircular arch. Overhead the rounded columns divide the elevation into a wide central bay with much narrower bays on either side. The central bay has a large semicircular sash window with small panes. This has a moulded arch with a carved keystone and side columns. In contrast, the windows of the outer bays are tall and slim. The same window pattern is repeated on the first floor without the central arch, but with carved garlands filling the space between the upper and lower windows of the outer bays. A deep entablature, or crosspiece, stretched across the heads of the columns, over which the richly decorated pediment supports a ball and flame finial. Unfortunately due to the enclosed position within the yard, views of the building are very restricted and there is no public access.

8. No. 24 Queen Square

The north side of Queen Square was laid out in the form of a symmetrically arranged Palladian block of seven houses. John Wood the Elder was the architect and work on the development started around 1728. No. 24 in the centre of the

The north block of Queen Square was laid out as a single unified Palladian composition with rustication, double-height columns and standard Georgian windows.

The pavilions that mark the ends of the north side of Queen Square were given an extra storey.

The central house on the north side of Queen Square projects slightly with curved columns and an elaborate triangular pediment.

block is the largest and is flanked on both sides by a pair of houses, with a further house at each end that act as terminating pavilions. The block is rusticated at ground level, above which flat double-height columns extend upwards to the parapet, with a first- and second-floor standard Georgian sash window positioned between each pair of columns. No. 24 projects slightly forward of the other houses. It has a central doorcase and five window bays across the front, with an elaborate triangular roof pediment complete with urns. The remainder of the houses are three window bays wide, with the side-by-side entrance doors to one side, and an attic storey and dormer windows at roof level. The end pavilion bays have an additional storey with square windows in place of the attic storey and dormer windows. The houses are separated from the footpath by the basement open area protected by the plain metal railings. The houses in the block are all in private ownership and public access is not available.

9. No. 15, Beauford Square

No. 15 Beauford Square is one of a range of uniform terraced houses that face the small central garden of the square. The architect was John Strahan and the house was built around 1730. The two-storey house has a basement and

Above: No. 15 Beauford Square is part of a coherent terrace of houses that face the garden of the square.

Left: The elevation of No. 15 Beauford Square displays a range of Georgian features including framed sash windows, side entrance door, elaborate eaves and an attic dormer. The blind window opening on the first floor, common to several houses on the square, is an unusual feature.

attic storey with dormer windows. The elevation is elaborate for a small house, with a plain metal railing that separates the house and basement area from the footpath. The ground floor has the doorway to one side, with side columns and a curved pediment supported by brackets. The two closely spaced sash windows have moulded surrounds and moulded pediments. The first-floor elevation of No. 15, and some of the other houses in the terrace, has an unusual window pattern. This includes three window openings, each with a moulded surround, but with one blind opening. An interesting feature of the blind window opening is the circular cut out that once held a clock face – a possible reference to the trade of the resident who once lived there. The house is a private residence and public access is not available.

10. No. 40 Gay Street

No.40 Gay Street offers an example of the standard Georgian town house so characteristic of Bath. It was laid out by John Woods the Elder around 1735 and forms part of a uniform terrace block that rises uphill in steps from Queen Square.

No. 40 Gay Street can be seen as representing a typical Georgian town house in Bath, part of a uniform terrace of similar houses.

The house is three storeys high with a basement and attic storey. The plain ashlar elevation has two vertically proportioned sash windows at ground level, above which the upper levels have three similar windows on each level with moulded cornices. The characteristic Georgian-style multiple glazing bars have, however, been replaced by a single pane in each sash. The basement has an open area to the front and this is protected by a metal railing that extends across the area to provide access to the door. This has a plain rectangular opening with side columns and a triangular pediment. Internally the accommodation has a double room layout on each floor: a room at the front and a room at the rear with the entrance hall and stairs to one side. The basement contained the kitchen, the ground and first floor the drawing rooms and the second and attic floors the bedrooms. Nowadays the house operates as the Jane Austin Centre with its museum and tearooms.

11. No. 41 Gay Street

No. 41 Gay Street was built for a merchant, Richard Martin, around 1735. The architect was John Wood the Elder and the end of terrace house was positioned on a corner site. The plain-fronted building is three storeys high over a basement with an unusual and elaborate semicircular corner bay at the junction with Old

No. 41 Gay Street is an end-of-terrace house positioned at the corner of Gay Street and Old King Street.

King Street. This elaborate bay extends to the full height of the building with the windows spaced around the curve on each floor. The ground and first-floor windows are framed with exaggerated block masonry jambs, with a Venetian, or tripartite, window on the first floor. This has a central round-headed opening with a closely spaced side light on either side. The doorcase on Gay Street is positioned to one side of the house. This has side columns, a semicircular arch, a fanlight and a flat moulded pediment. The small but interesting keystone over the arch is in the shape of a grotesque face. Internally the house has an unusual plan. It has a large oval room on each floor reflected in the curve of the semicircular bay window. The house is in business use with no public access.

The three-storey circular bay window of No. 41 Gay Street with its sash windows and solid block jambs highlights the corner position of the house.

The semicircular doorcase of No. 41 Gay Street has rounded columns and a flat pediment. The keystone over the arched fanlight is in the form of a grotesque face.

12. No. 20 The Circus

The Circus consists of three independent curved blocks of uniform terraced houses arranged to form a circle around a central landscaped green. Built in 1754, the original layout was designed by the architect John Wood the Elder, but completed by his son, John Wood the Younger. No.20 is typical of the uniform elevation of the remainder of the houses in the development and stands three storeys high with a basement and attic storey. The individual floor levels and roof line are marked by a richly carved cornice as well as a solid parapet overhead. This is punctuated by oval apertures that allow daylight into the attic windows. The house has three sash window bays on each floor, each separated from one another by double columns on each of the three levels. The first-floor windows alone have a continuous trellised balcony. The basement area is separated from the wide footpath by plain metal railings. These stretch across the front of the house and lead across the bridge over the area to a rectangular doorcase set between double columns. Internally the layout follows the standard town house plan: a room to the front and a room to the rear. The house is in private ownership with no public access.

Above: The Circus has three curved uniform terraced blocks arranged around the central landscaped garden.

Right: The doorway of No. 20 The Circus is flanked by double columns with a rectangular fanlight.

No. 20 The Circus has a sequence of double columns with sash windows set between each pair on each of the three floors.

13. No. 21 Brock Street

No. 21 Brock Street sits near the middle of a uniform terrace of eighteenth-century houses on the north side of the street, between the Circus and the Royal Crescent. The house was designed by John Wood the Younger around 1763 and stands

No. 21 sits into the uniform terraced Georgian streetscape of Brock Street.

No. 21 Brock Street has a range of Georgian sash and Venetian windows on all floors and an open pedimented doorcase at ground level.

three storeys high with a basement and an attic. The ground floor has a slightly projecting pedimented doorcase, plain railings and a pair of standard windows to one side. Overhead the first and second floors each have Venetian-type windows that feature a round-headed sash closely flanked on either side by narrow sashes. The house is in private ownership with no public access.

14. No. 38/39 Somersetshire Buildings, Milsom Street

No. 38/39 Somersetshire Building is part of a Palladian-fronted block of uniform houses designed by Thomas Baldwin around 1766 and built on the site of a former poorhouse. The building was occupied by the Bath and Somerset Bank in 1783, Stuckey's Bank in 1859 and is now a branch of the National and Westminster Bank. The dramatic three-storey building opens directly onto the street and has a wide semicircular full-height bay, flanked on both sides by a single narrow bay. The ground floor is rusticated with three round-headed windows in the curve of the bay. The building originally had a round-headed door on each side of the bay, but on the south side that was later changed to a window to match the windows of the bay. The first and second floors have a sequence of double-storey columns

Above: No. 38/39 Somersetshire Building acts as the central house within a wide palace fronted uniform block on Milsom Street.

Left: The semi-circular bay of 38/39 Somersetshire Buildings extends for the full height of the building with three sash windows on each floor.

with a sash window between each pair. Overhead the line of the deep moulded and balustraded cornice follows the curve of the bay. The ground floor of the building is now in banking use with partial access to the public.

15. No. 1 Royal Crescent

The Royal Crescent is one of the major set pieces of Georgian architecture and town planning in Bath and consists of thirty uniform Palladian terraced houses laid out in the form of a half ellipse that faces onto a landscaped park. The crescent was designed by John Wood the Younger and was laid out in 1767. No. 1 was leased to various tenants and over the years acted as a school for young ladies and a lodging house. In 1968 the house and the adjoining service wing were separated, but later, following restoration work, the service area was reintegrated and the house was opened as a museum. The crescent front of the house stands three storeys high with a basement and an attic in the roof. The ground level has three sash windows set into the ashlar masonry. Overhead, the sash windows on the first and second floors are set between round columns, while the roofline is highlighted by a deep moulded cornice. In contrast to the other houses on the crescent, the doorcase of No. 1 is on the end of the building facing onto Brock Street. Here the elevation design is similar to the main front with five window bays on each floor. Today the house acts as a museum where the restored eighteenth-century interiors can be appreciated.

No. 1, with its Palladian elevation, terminates the east side of the Royal Crescent.

Left: The symmetrical Brock Street elevation of No. 1 Royal Crescent has a central doorcase flanked on each side by two sash windows and five windows set between columns on the upper floors.

Below: No. 1 Royal Crescent offers a range of restored eighteenth-century house interiors.

16. Pulteney Bridge

Pulteney Bridge was built in 1769 to facilitate access to the development of the Bathwick estate lands on the far side of the River Avon. The architect was Robert Adam and the bridge spanned the river in three semicircular arches. At street level both sides of the bridge are lined with a parade of retail units, although the down-river side is the more elaborate. Here there is a double-storey central bay with a tall Venetian window and a broken pediment at roof level. In addition, the two end pavilions also have Venetian windows with domed roofs. The shop units between the bays have box-type shopfronts with side columns and fascias. In contrast, the shops on the opposite side of the bridge all have plain uniform box frame shopfronts. Initially the shop units were single storey in structure, but a small first floor level was added to these in 1792.

Pulteney Bridge spans the River Avon in three wide semicircular arches.

Above: The middle and end bays of Pulteney Bridge have Venetian windows set within semicircular arches.

Below: The majority of the Pulteney Bridge shops have box-framed shopfronts with side columns and fascias.

17. The Assembly Rooms, Bennett Street

The Assembly Rooms in Bennett Street was designed by the architect John Wood the Younger and built in 1769. This is an elegant venue where many of the social events of eighteenth-century Bath, such as balls and card games, were celebrated. The Rooms, although initially successful, went slowly into decline and were converted into a cinema in 1921. Ten years later the building was restored and taken over by the National Trust. In 1942, the building suffered badly from bomb damage, but was restored in 1956. In 1963, the Museum of Costume was opened in the basement and in 1987 the building was further restored and opened to the public. The Assembley Rooms block is a mixture of single- and double-height elements. The Bennett Street elevation, for example, has a single-storey arcade of arched windows and a row of sash windows on the main building immediately behind. In contrast, the Alfred Street side has three rows of standard sash windows. The single-storey projecting main entrance portico faces onto Saville Row and is in the form of an open Greco-Roman temple front. This has four circular columns supporting an entablature or beam, with an overhead triangular pediment. Internally the building accommodation consists of three large assembly rooms laid out in a U-shaped arrangement around an octagonal hall: the Ball Room, the octagonal Card Room and the Tea Room, with an upper gallery at one end.

The single-storey entrance to the Assembly Rooms is in the form of a Greco-Roman temple front.

Left: The Bennett Street elevation of the Assembly Rooms has a single-storey arcade of arched windows and a high-level row of sash windows on the main building immediately behind.

Below: The octagonal Card Room of the Assembly Rooms with high-level windows.

18. Former New Prison, Grove Street

In around 1769 St Mary's Church was demolished to facilitate the erection of Pulteney Bridge so as to provide access to the lands on the east side of the River Avon. The church tower acted as the city prison and in order to compensate for the loss of the prison accommodation, William Pulteney built a new prison on Grove Street in 1772. The prison went out of use around 1842 and the building was later used as a police barracks and as tenements, and in 1972 it was converted to residential apartments. The building was designed by the architect Thomas Warr Atwood in the form of an elegant three-storey symmetrical Palladian building over a basement. This was divided into three bays, with the outer bays projecting slightly. The building has five sash windows across the front, of which the first-floor windows have triangular pediments. The first-and second-level masonry was plain ashlar, beneath which the ground level was rusticated. At roof level a balustrade-type pediment stretched across the full width of the building. At some period in the past, the street level was dropped and the original steps to the entrance were removed. The ashlar faced basement then became, in effect, the ground level – a juxtaposition of levels that reduced to some degree the initial Palladian intention of the architect. The building is now in private residential use with no access to the general public.

The former New Prison with its rusticated and plain ashlar masonry.

19. The Guildhall, High Street

The Guildhall was laid out on the east side of High Street in two separate stages. In 1775, the architect Thomas Baldwin laid out the initial stage in the form of a three-bay symmetrical Palladian block. The centre bay is rusticated at ground level with an arched doorway flanked by arched windows. Overhead the three sash windows on the first and second floor are set between rounded columns, on top of which a triangular pediment displays the city's coat of arms and a figure of Justice. The side bays have a single window on the ground and first floors. In 1891, the second stage of the Guildhall was laid out by the architect John McKean Brydon. Here a pair of side wings with rounded end pavilions was added to the Baldwin's initial block. The wings are two storeys high with four windows on each level. The ground level is rusticated with the windows set into semicircular arches. The end pavilions are taller with a framed doorway and a domed cupola on the roof. In addition, the three-storey rounded ends of the pavilions curve into Beridge Street and Orange Grove, respectively. Two years later, Brydon was responsible for the shallow dome that was placed on the roof of the original block. Today the Guildhall presents a dynamic streetscape along the length of High Street. The Guildhall houses the city administration and is partially accessible to the public.

The Palladian elevation of the earliest phase of the Guildhall laid out by Thomas Baldwin.

Above: The curved end of the pavilion that turns into Bridge Street was the second stage in the completion of the Guildhall.

Below: The complete block of the Guildhall fills the east side of the High Street.

20. Hot Bath, Hot Bath Street

The square single-storey Hot Bath building was designed by John Wood the Younger and was built in 1775. This was originally a free-standing building with a flat roof and short splayed corners that housed a central octagonal bath and a system of lobbies and dressing rooms. The original layout was considerably altered in 1925 and again in 1999 and is now integrated into the New Royal Bath designed by Donald Insall Associates, architects, and Nicholas Grimshaw and Partners, architects – from where it is open to the public. Today the original doors and windows have been much changed, although the original entrance porch opening onto Hot Bath Street survives, although unused. The open entrance porch is very similar to the Assembly Rooms buildings entrance porch (Building 17), also designed by John Wood the Younger, and consists of a Greco-Roman temple-style portico with four circular columns, an entablature and a triangular pediment, flanked on both sides by a pair of sash windows.

The original Hot Bath temple-style entrance portico and windows face onto Hot Bath Street.

21. St Swithin's Church, the Paragon

St Swithin's Church was designed by the architects Jelly and Palmer and was built in 1777 on the site of a tenth-century church, the foundations of which can still be seen in the crypt. Uniquely, it is the only Georgian-style church still in use in Bath. The side elevation has a sequence of seven flat full-height columns with a low-level and upper-level window spaced between each pair. The front elevation is more elaborate with its tall three stack west tower. This has a square base, an arched doorway with columns and a portico, a clock, a bracketed pediment on the ground level, a louvered belfry on the second level and an octagonal base and spire on the top level – all rising one above the other. In addition, a low-level side gallery, with a sash window, flank each side of the tower. Internally the church has an upper level gallery, double-height columns, and double-tier windows. Among the notable individuals with links to the church are Jane Austen and William Wilberforce.

The side elevation of St Swithin's Church has a pattern of six windows set between full-height columns.

The tall three-tier west tower dominates the street elevation of St Swithin's Church.

22. Cross Bath, Bath Street

Cross Bath is a small free-standing single-storey pump room, or bathhouse, fitted into a tight site at the west end of Bath Street, designed by the city architect Thomas Baldwin in 1783. In 1792 John Palmer, the subsequent city architect, demolished the building and rebuilt it along the same lines, effectively aligning the iconic building with the central axis of Bath Street. In 1829, 1854 and 1885 the building experienced considerable alterations. In 1999, the architects, Nicholas Grimshaw and Partners and Donald Insall Associates, completed a restoration of the building. This included an open-air spa and a flat-roofed entrance lobby. Today the elevations of the building are complex, despite its small scale. The east side presents a closing vista to Bath Street. This has a partially bowed front divided into three bays by columns, a raised plaque at roof level with urns and an overhead panel with a pedestal inset. The elevation retains some original window and door openings, which are now blocked up. The south elevation follows a similar rhythm. It is curved at one side with a pattern of columns and solid window openings. The north elevation is quite different. It has an open semicircular porch, originally added by Palmer, with four round columns and a central doorway.

This aeriel view of the restored Cross Bath Spa shows the open pool and covered entrance porch. (Permission from Donald Insall Associates Architects to reproduce this image is gratefully acknowledged)

The east elevation of Cross Bath Spa acts as a closing vista to Cross Bath Street.

23. Grand Pump Room, Abbey Church Yard

The Grand Pump Room was built in 1791 and acted as Bath city's main civic building where visitors came to take the waters. The building was initially designed by the city architect Thomas Baldwin and completed by his successor John Palmer. The Grand Pump Room, when taken together with the adjoining Concert Room, Great Bath pool and the museum, forms an integral part of the Roman Bath complex. The building has a complex elevation with a seven-window central bay and two end pavilions that front onto Abbey Church Yard. The double-height central bay has seven windows across the front, and incorporates an attached double-height portico with four half-round columns and a high-level triangular pediment as well as an off-centre doorway at ground level. The tall lower-level sash windows are placed between the columns, with small elliptical overhead windows set into rectangular openings. The east pavilion has a slight forward projection, with a temple front porch at ground level and an elaborate round-headed window overhead. The west pavilion is similar except at ground level, where the porch has been replaced by one end of the Abbey Church Yard colonnade. Today, the building functions as a restaurant where visitors can dine and view the old Roman Baths from the rear windows. Internally the large double-storey dining area is rectangular in layout with an arched semicircular apse at each end.

Above: The complex elevation of the Grand Pump Room faces out onto Abbey Church Yard.

Below: The double-height Grand Pump Room restaurant has an arched semicircular apse at each end.

24. Nos 5 and 6, the Colonnade, Bath Street

The laying out of Bath Street by Thomas Baldwin in 1791 was a major set piece in Georgian town planning and consisted of a north/south axial street, with the central axis aligned on Kings Bath on Stall Street at one end and Cross Bath at the opposite end, so as to provide both streets with a closing vista. In addition, each end of the streets opens out in a semicircular space. The buildings that line both sides of the street are three-storey houses with a dormer roof and retail accommodation at ground level. Although the units on the north side of the street were combined in 1988 and now act as a single retail store. The most significant feature of the project is, however, the open colonnade that stretches along both sides of the street. Here the shopfronts are set back from the building line with the overhead structure carried on colonnades of slim circular uprights. The reason for this was to provide shelter for visitors while they waited to use the baths. The ground floor of the south side of the street was partially restored between 1963 and 1990 and Units 5 and 6 have had reproduction eighteenth-century shopfronts inserted. On the upper level the window pattern has sash windows on the first and second levels, with a triangular pediment on every third window and a string course that divides the floors from one another. The shop units are accessible to the public, but the upper levels are in private use with no public access.

The King's Bath provided a closing vista to the colonnaded Bath Street.

Nos 5 and 6
Bath Street has
had reproduction
eighteenth-century
shopfronts inserted.

25. No. 19 Northampton Street

No. 29 is one of a number of terraced houses built on the steep end of Northampton Street around 1820. The narrow house was designed by the architect George Phillips Manners and is three storeys high over a basement, although the top floor was a later addition. The street elevation has a plain ashlar front with a projecting

No. 19 Northampton Street is part of a stepped terrace of houses that echo the rise of the street.

No. 19 Northampton Street opens directly off the footpath with the head of the basement window protruding slightly above the footpath level.

cornice between the first and top floor that marks the original height of the building. The house lacks an open basement area and, unusually, only the tip of the basement window protrudes above the footpath level. The doorway is set into a plain arched opening with a single ground-floor window beside it. Overhead the upper floors have a pair of windows on each level and a plain parapet at roof level. The house has a charming domestic atmosphere enhanced by the flower boxes on the ground and first-floor windows. The premises is a private dwelling with no access to the public.

26. Holburne Museum of Art, Great Pulteney Street

The Holburne Museum is a symmetrical Palladian-style building laid out by the architect Charles Harcourt Masters in 1796 as a tavern and was part of the Sydney Gardens public facilities. In 1836, the building housed a hotel and in 1853 it was used as a college. In 1911, the building was converted into a gallery to house the William Holburne art collection and 1916 the collection was opened to the public. Later, in 2011, an extensive extension in a twentieth-century idiom was added to the rear to cater for the museum's growing collection (Building 49). The position of the museum was carefully chosen and was positioned at the end of, and on the central axis of, Great Pulteney Street, so as to present a dramatic closing vista to the street. The three-storey elevation facing the axis is divided into three bays. The ground level of the projecting central bay is rusticated with three semicircular entrance arches. Above this the second floor has a tall four column temple front with three sash windows positioned between the columns and a triangular pediment at the second floor. The side bays have three windows of varying height on each level, above which the parapet has a sequence of urns. The interior of the museum has been the subject of much modification since 1796 and today the layout consists of a series of display galleries on all three floors, in addition to which a library and archive were added at basement level in 2011.

The Holburne Museum is positioned on the central axis of Great Pulteney Street and presents a closing vista to the street.

The Palladian elevation of the Holburne Museum faces down Great Pulteney Street.

27. Shop and House, No. 8 Argyle Street

No. 8 Argyle Street is part of a uniform terrace of shops with accommodation overhead. The house was built on an angled site at the intersection of Laura Place and Argyle Street around 1800 and the architect was Thomas Baldwin. The building is three storeys high with a basement and attic storey. Shortly after the house was built, possibly around 1827, a projected shopfront was added to the Argyle Street elevation. The basement area was floored over and the shopfront, with its remarkably elegant design, was built over the area. Each of the doorways on either side is flanked by circular columns and the central display window is divided into rectangular panes. Overhead, the full-width fascia and cornice is inscribed with the name 'A. H. Hall'. A most unusual feature is the coloured representation of the royal arms of Queen Charlotte placed on top of the fascia. Today the shop is in use as pharmacy. Overhead the plain ashlar upper floors have a pair of sash windows on each level, with a blank opening between each pair. The first floor opening is semicircular with flat bracketed pediment, while the top floor opening is plain. Above this, the building is spanned by a triangular roofline pediment, which hides the attic windows.

Above: No. 8 Argyle Street is part of a uniform block of shops and houses and marks the corner of Laura Place and Argyle Street.

Below: The shopfront of No. 8 Argyle carries the arms of Queen Charlotte.

The projecting elegant shopfront of No. 8 Argyle Street opens directly off the footpath.

28. Shop and House, No. 7 Old Bond Street

No. 7 Old Bond is one of a terrace of six houses with shopfronts that open onto the narrow pedestrian street. Although the house dates from around 1760, the shopfront to No. 7 seems to have been added around 1800. This has a central doorway flanked on either side by projecting bow-shaped display windows. Each of the bows is supported with the help of a single metal stub beneath each window. The whole composition is set between side columns, each with a miniature lion's head, as well as a fascia that follows the curved line of the double bow. Unfortunately the original glazing bars have been replaced with mullions. Above the shopfront, the upper floor originally had a first-floor Venetian window. This has, however, been replaced by sashes of unequal size and a metal window balcony. The adjoining shopfront at No 8 has a similar double bow window, with the surviving glazing bars.

Side-by-side double-bow shopfronts on Old Bond Street.

The double-bow
shopfront of No. 7
Old Bond Street
supported by
low-level metal stubs.

29. Theatre Royal, Beauford Square

Facing south onto the landscaping of Beauford Square, the Theatre Royal was
built in 1802 to the design of George Dance the Younger, although the building
work was completed by the architect George Palmer. The building suffered a
fire in 1862. The interior was repaired and at the same time the entrance was

The former front elevation of the Theatre Royal, with its extended ground-level podium
and old entrance door overlooking Beauford Square.

moved from Beauford Square to Saw Close. The building is three storeys high and was built against the taller blank wall of the main auditorium. The ground-level podium is the widest part of the elevation and extends across nine curved window openings, with the original entrance door in the centre. Overhead the two upper floors are narrower with five window bays across the front. This has six plain hollow columns with a single sash window between the columns on each level. Each of the columns is topped by a theatrical mask with a garland between each mask. Overhead the projecting parapet carries the royal Hanoverian arms and four stylistic lyres all projecting the idea of the theatre and its royal connection.

30. No. 1 Sydney Place

No. 1 on Sydney Place was designed by the architect John Pinch the Elder and dates from 1804. The house is at one end of a pair of uniform terrace that face the Holburne Museum across the road, with three floors, a basement and an attic storey. The street elevation is conventional, with three round headed windows

Sydney Place Terrace with No. 1 at one end.

The front corner tower, entrance porch and first-floor balcony of No. 1 Sydney Terrace.

The side elevation of No. 1 Sydney Terrace with the pair of corner towers.

at ground level, rectangular sash windows on the first and second floor and a projecting band between the two floor levels. The attic floor projects slightly forward and has a triangular pediment overhead. The remarkable feature of the house is the side elevation, with a pair of round towers at each corner, joined by the projecting bands carried around from the front elevation. The front tower has a projecting rectangular entrance porch, with a round-headed door and side windows, double corner columns, and a first-floor balcony, as well as a blank niche on each side of the tower. Overhead the tower has three sash windows on each of the upper floors. The back corner tower is similar, but with two sash windows on each floor level, while between the towers there are two windows on each level. The overall impact of the house, particularly if viewed from the side, is surprising and perhaps more suggestive of the Scottish Baronial than Georgian Bath. The house is in private ownership with no public access. No 4, on the adjoining Sydney Parade block, was the home of the writer Jane Austin between 1001 and 1807.

31. No. 7 Northumberland Place

No. 7 Northumberland Place is one of a parade of four small double-storey similar shop units laid out around 1830 and entered through an archway from the adjoining High Street and when considered together the parade of shops

Above: The parade of four shopfronts facing onto Northumberland Place.

Left: The projecting square shopfront of No. 7 Northumberland Place.

has an intrinsic unitary value. The square bay shopfront on the ground level is supported on brackets, with the doorway to one side and a slim fascia overhead. The entire shopfront is framed between a pair of narrow columns, each with a lion mask at the top and is now colour washed, as are the rest of the parade fronts. Unfortunately some of the vertical glazing bars on No. 7 have been removed. On the upper level, No. 7 has a single sash window and a plain parapet shielding the roof.

32. The Bazaar, No. 9 Quiet Street

The Bazaar was designed by Henry Edmond Goodridge and dates from 1824. The building originally represented the central bay of the Auction Market and Bazaar that stretched between Nos 7–11. The building once held a Methodist chapel and is now occupied by a branch of the Royal Bank of Scotland at ground level. The tri-part building has a wide modern-looking display window at ground level. This is flanked by rusticated panel work, although the original plain ashlar first-floor elevation survives intact. Here the central tripartite window has balusters underneath and a semicircular fanlight over it. The window is flanked on either side by blank niches with figure sculptures representing Commerce and Genius, and sunken rectangular panels at the base. The plain parapet has three

The Bazaar sits into the continuous streetscape of Quiet Street.

The elevation of the Bazaar offers
a range of Georgian architectural
elements including a tripartite
window, semicircular fanlight,
niches and figure sculpture.

stepped bays and features a rooftop figure sculpture. Taken together, the Venetian window, fanlight, niches, and figure sculpture combine to set the building apart. Overall the building represents the finest examples of Bath's nineteenth-century commercial street architecture. Today the building is in bank use with partial access to the public.

33. No. 24 Great Stanhope Street

No. 24 Great Stanhope Street was designed by Edward Davis around 1830. Davis was clearly influenced by the architect Sir John Soane in his design of a number of elements. These include the entrance porch and balcony railings. The house is part of a uniform terrace of three-storey houses with two sash window bays per house, basements, basement areas, and attic storeys, although No. 24 has a number of features not shared by the other houses in the terrace. The ground-floor wall is rusticated and the house has a projecting entrance

Below left: No. 24 is set into the uniform streetscape of Great Stanhope Street.

Below right: The form and geometric designs of the No. 24 Great Stanhope Street porch reflects the influence of the architect Sir John Soane.

The rear extension and high-level terrace at the rear of No. 24 Great Stanhope Street.

porch, whereas the other houses have plain ashlar and applied doorcases with triangular pediments. The ground-floor window of No. 24 is round headed and the corresponding rectangular windows on the upper levels have metal balconies. The flat-roofed porch has double doors, slim rectangular side columns, a flat roof and blank niches on both sides, very much in the mode of Sir John Soane. Internally the layout has the standard eighteenth-century double room arrangement with the entrance hall and stairs to one side. In an unusual case, the depth of the house was increased by several metres shortly after it was built, on the basement, ground and first floors. Today the roof of the extension acts as a high-level landscaped patio. The house is in private residential use with no access to the public.

34. Nightwatchmen's Sentry Boxes, Great Pulteney Street

At the eastern end of Great Pulteney Street two nightwatchmen's sentry boxes flank the entrance to the Holburne Museum, face down the street and contribute to the axial layout. Both boxes are identical, dating from 1830, and provided shelter for watchmen who acted as the city's nightwatch patrol prior to the establishment of Sir Robert Peeler's police force in 1829. The stone boxes are 3 metres high, around a metre square, open at the front, with a stone bench internally, flat columns on the street face, and a flat stone roof – much like a pair of miniature temples. Another sentry box also survives adjacent to Norfolk Crescent. Here the shape of the box is circular, with the door on one face as well as flat columns and a flat dome. All three are unusual survivors from the eighteenth century and, despite their small scale, display a high level of Georgian architectural detail.

Below left: The stone-built nightwatchman's small sentry box faces down Great Pulteney Street.

Below right: The circular nightwatchman's sentry box adjacent to Norfolk Crescent.

35. New Jerusalem Church, Henry Street

The New Church, which followed the Swedenborgianism ideals, was designed by the architect Henry Underwood and, according to the date stone, was built in 1844, where Isaac Pitman, the inventor of the method of shorthand was once a member of the congregation. The design features a handsome double-height temple front with a basement, set on a plain raised plinth. The temple front is divided into three main bays by four three-quarter columns and a pair of subsidiary outer bays marked by two flat end columns. The ground-level walling over the plinth is rusticated with the central doorcase in the middle bay. This has a moulded frame and a flat moulded hood, over which is the framed 1844 date stone plaque. The first floor level is plain ashlar, with a pair of tall round-headed window set between the three-quarter columns. The entablature, or cross-beam, stretches across the heads of the columns and caries the triangular pediment that matches the roofline. The interior of the church has recently been extensively renovated. It is now in office use and there is no access to the general public.

The imposing temple front of the New Church is a notable streetscape element of Henry Street.

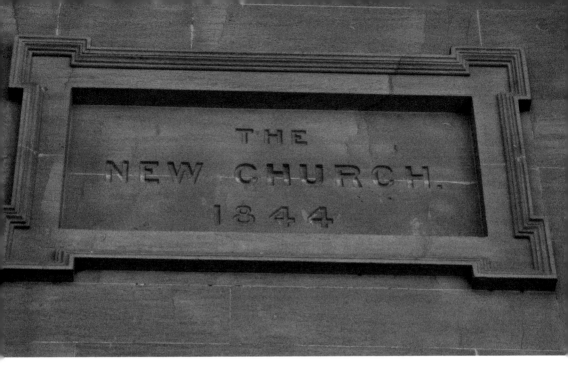

Framed 1844 date stone plaque of the New Church.

36. Former Central Police Station and Magistrates' Court, Orange Grove

The Former Central Police Station dates from 1865 and was designed by the architect Charles Edward Davis. In 1998 the station was closed and the building was converted for use as a restaurant, while retaining the street elevation. The design of the double-storey building follows an Italianate style and stands boldly between the Guildhall and the Empire Hotel. The ground floor is rusticated with three tall round-headed windows and a door to one side. The upper floor is plain ashlar with three large round-headed windows. Overhead the roof is projected outwards on brackets. During the conversion the interior was considerably altered. Immediately on the west side of the station is the gateway to the Guildhall courtyard. The gateways resembles a Roman triumphal arch, with a large central archway flanked by a pair of smaller and lower pedestrian gateways – each with an open oculus overhead. The arches are highlighted with staggered masonry blocks and keystones, with open balustrade stretching along the top. Taken together the station and the gateway make an attractive backdrop to the landscape of Orange Grove, where the Beau Nash's central obelisk marks the visit of the Prince of Orange to Bath in 1734. Behind the Former Police Station, but almost unknown, is the only surviving remains of the medieval East Gate of the city. Here the arched gateway is located on Stall Boat Lane. The current lane is around 6 metres above the original medieval street level, so that the gate is almost hidden in a hole. Nevertheless it presents a remarkable survival from the city's past.

Above: The front elevation of the former Central Police Station with its bold masonry work and arched openings.

Below: The rounded opening of the Guildhall gateway and former Central Police Station act as a visual reinforcement to one another.

The remains of the City Gate, visible below street level on Stall Boat Lane, is a rare visual representation of Bath's medieval past.

37. Former Concert Room, Abbey Church Yard

Although dating from well into the Victorian era, the Concert Room is spatially and architecturally linked to the adjacent Grand Pump Room, and together contribute to the Roman Bath Museum. The single gallery room was designed by the architect John McKeane Brydon and built in 1897. Originally envisaged as a concert room, the building proved unsuitable for concerts and now acts as a reception area to the museum. Brydon's double-storey complex symmetrical elevation faces onto Abbey Church Yard. It has a rusticated ground floor with a central square-headed doorway flanked by narrow sash windows. The upper level has a three-bay portico with semicircular columns and an overhead triangular pediment. The central bay at this level has an arched Venetian window between the columns while the outer bays have blank niches with bracketed pediments over. Both the window and niches have balustrades at their bases. On either side of the main block is a single-level passageway. One extends around the corner to Kingston Parade and on the opposite side the other links the concert room directly with the adjoining Grand Pump Room. Internally the double-height reception gallery features a range of Georgian features including the coffered dome, apses and half domes and provides access to the Great Bath and museum beyond.

The imposing symmetrical elevation of the former Concert Room faces onto Abbey Church Yard.

The central bay of the former Concert Room, with the entrance doorway, Venetian window and overhead pediment.

The upper and lower gallery of the Great Bath pool accessed from the Concert Room.

38. Temple of Minerva, Royal Victoria Park

The Temple of Minerva began as the City of Bath Pavilion at the British Empire Exhibition in Wembley in 1924 and 25. It was designed by the architect Alfred Taylor and re-erected beside the kidney-shaped pool in the Royal Victoria Park

The Temple of Minerva with the inscribed parapet is positioned looking down on a kidney-shaped pool and surrounded by a rich landscape.

The sides of the Temple of Minerva have a Venetian-type window and 'CITY OF BATH' inscribed on the parapet.

Botanic Gardens in 1926. The single-storey rectangular building measures 6 metres by 5 metres internally and originally had three arched openings facing the pool and a tripartite Venetian-type window on the side elevation, although the arches were later closed in with glazed doors. The roof is defined by a moulded cornice with a plain parapet over. The front parapet carries the Latin inscription '*AQUAE SULIS*' (The Roman name for Bath), while the side parapet is inscribed 'CITY OF BATH'. The temple is one of the last contributions to the Georgian building movement of Bath and is currently used for weddings or other public receptions.

39. Countess of Huntingdon's Chapel, The Vineyards (Building of Bath Museum)

The Countess of Huntingdon's Chapel was built by the countess in 1765 as a Methodist chapel, although it later functioned as a Presbyterian church until 1981, when it was last used for religious purposes. In 1984, the building was restored by the Bath Preservation Trust and opened as the Building of Bath Museum. This explores the history and development of the city's eighteenth-century architecture. The building was one of the earliest exercises in the Gothic Revival style to appear

The tripartite windows of the Countess of Huntingdon's Chapel with ogee heads.

The Countess of Huntingdon's Chapel with its Gothic Revival features including the ogee windows and battlements.

in Bath and resembles nothing as much as a miniature medieval castle, with Gothic windows and rooftop battlements. The plain double-height chapel is positioned at the rear of the building, while the front section, which provided residential accommodation, faces onto the street. This was initially the countess's home, but was later used by the serving clergymen. The central bay of the building is double storied over a basement and is flanked on each side by single-storey wings. The striking feature of the building is the Gothic Revival windows. The main double-storey canted bay has a central tripartite window on each level, flanked by narrow sidelights on the splay of the cant. These have a vertical emphasis with ogee, or double-curved heads. The paired windows on the wings are wider, again with ogee heads. The short front garden is separated from the outside footpath by metal arrowhead railings and a pair of comparative metal gates with swan-necked archways over them.

4c. Park Farm House, Royal Victoria Park

In his design for Park Farm House, the architect Edward Davis chose the Picturesque style with the idea of recreating his image of what a Gothic farmhouse should look like. The house was initially a pair of cottages and only later was it converted into a single dwelling. Today the house sits in the countryside

Above: The irregular massing of Park Farm House sits against the wooded background of Victoria Park.

Left: The entrance porch to Park Farm has a curved doorcase, an 1831 date stone and steep highly decorated bargeboards.

atmosphere of Victoria Park surrounded by mature trees. The irregular mass of the house is double storey in height and is arranged in an L-shaped form with a range of different scale front-facing gables, each with a heavily decorated bargeboard. The off-centre entrance porch has an elliptical doorcase with the 1831 date stone cut into a recessed panel over the door. The mullioned windows throughout the house vary considerably in scale and levels. These include tripartite and double-pane examples as well as a first-floor oriel, or bay, window – all with overhead protecting hoods. A set of tall chimney stacks with octagonal shafts crown the steep slated roof to complete the image of the rural antique.

41. Bath Spa Railway Station, Dorchester Street

When Isambard Kingdom Brunel built Bath Spa railway station, as part of the Great Western Railway system in 1841, he based the design of the station building on a version of the Jacobean Revival. Brunel carefully positioned the station block so that it faced north and provided a closing vista to the Manvers Street approach. The train shed originally had a glass roof but this was replaced by the present canopy in 1885. The double-storey station building was laid out on an irregular building line with a curved section and a projecting pavilion to one side. This has a projecting entrance bay with Dutch gables and a clock face on the roofline.

The irregular entrance elevation of the Jacobean Revival-style Bath Spa railway station.

The glazed entrance canopy of Bath Spa railway station.

The ground level has an arcade of semicircular doorways with decorated fanlights that stretch across the front, except for the pavilion that has a doorway flanked by two round headed windows. The semicircular doorways were originally open until the current doors were installed in the twentieth century. The first floor level has a continuous line of mullioned windows with a mixture of different size panes. The glazed canopy with its metal-framed support that extends across the main entrance section of the building was added in the 1880s. Internally the entrance, through the arched arcade, is on ground level with a stairs and lift to the station offices and platforms on the first floor.

42. St John the Evangelist Church, South Park

St John's Church was built in 1861 initially as a Benedictine priory. The building was laid out in the Gothic Revival style and was designed by the architect Charles Francis Hansom. The monks withdrew from Bath in 1932 and the church was handed over to Bath's Roman Catholic parish. Hansom's design incorporates most of the characteristic elements of the Gothic Revival. These include an irregular layout, projecting bays, rough Bath stone masonry, buttresses, tall Gothic arched

St John the Evangelist Church projects all the characteristic features of the Gothic Revival.

The tall tower of St John's Church has a bold impact on the skyline of south Bath.

The transparent wrought-iron and brass rood screen of St John's Church divides the nave from the chancel.

windows and doors, a rose window, roof gables, a high-pitched slated roof, and a tall tower. The latter has three clear levels. The lower level has the main doorway, over which the tall pointed west window has elaborate tracery. The second, or belfry level, has large belfry windows on each face with louvers, while the top level has a tall octagonal stone spire. The result is a striking silhouette that offers a counterpoint to the uniformity of the Georgian city skyline, particularly when seen from the south. Internally the nave is divided from the side aisles by an arcade of pointed arches with high level windows over. The ceiling has pattern of decorated panels that date from repairs to the church after Second World War bombing. One of the significant features of the interior is, however, the rood screen. This was a common feature of medieval churches that divided the nave from the chancel, although the delicate wrought-iron and brass screen in St John's was designed by Agustus Welby Pugin in 1905 and restored in 2017.

43. Former Green Park Railway Station, Green Park Road

Green Park railway station is in effect a pair of interconnected buildings: the station entrance block with the train shed immediately behind. The building was designed for the Midland Railway by the architect J. H. Saunders and work on the construction started in 1868, although the station was closed just short of 100 years later.

Above: The formal entrance block to Green Park station acknowledges the Georgian character of Bath and is now in use as a restaurant and functions area.

Below: The riveted metal beams and columns span the train shed of Green Park station and carry the glazed roof over it.

The former Green Park station train shed with its curved metal and glazed roof is used for parking and as a market area.

The building was purchased by Bath City Council in 1974 and was restored for commercial use by the architects Stride Treglown in 1982. Saunders related his design of the station block on a traditional Georgian Bath model. This had a central bay flanked by end pavilions. The ground floor was given a rusticated finish, a sequence of doors and sash windows, and an ornate metal entrance porch that stretched across the central bay. The first floor is more elaborate with the five tall windows set between six columns and a Venetian window in each of side bays. Overhead a parapet of open balusters extends across the full width of the block. The long train shed immediately behind the station block has a span of 20 metres and was designed by J. S. Crossley, chief engineer of the Midland Railway. The imposing glazed curved roof is carried on fourteen riveted metal beams each supported on cast-iron columns. Today the station block acts as a restaurant with public rooms. The train shed platforms have been removed and shops have been laid out along one side. The large open central area of the shed now acts as a car park, with occasional use as a market.

44. Former Bath City Laundry, York Street

Bath City Laundry lies at the junction of York Street and Swallow Street and is one of the few historic industrial buildings of Bath to survive to the present day. The building dates from 1887 and was designed by the architect

The Bath City Laundry
chimney consists of a
slender circular shaft
extending upwards from
an arched and open base.

Above: The York Street elevation of Bath City Laundry has an arrangement of windows set between columns on the ground and first floor.

Below: The Bath City Laundry viaduct spans York Street and originally supplied hot water from Queen's Bath.

Charles Edward Davis. Historically it went through a number of uses including a chapel and a restaurant, although today there is a proposal to use the building as a museum. The York Street elevation is double storey with four round-headed windows and a flat-headed door to one side at ground level. Each of the windows and the door is set between flat columns. On the first floor five almost square windows are set between columns. These are similar to the ground-level columns except for the addition of elaborate bases carved in the shape of animal heads. Around the corner in Swallow Street the elevation is plain except for the grandiose side door. This has an elaborate broken pediment positioned over a wide curved arch and double doors. The building has, however, two unique features: a connecting viaduct and an elaborate chimney stack. The arched viaduct extends across York Street at high level and originally provided hot water to the laundry from the spring in the Queen's Bath. The arch is elliptical and is decorated with mouldings and a central triangular pediment. Visible only from Swallow Street, the laundry chimney has a tall circular shaft rising from a square base. The base has an open arch on each face and a triangular pediment. Currently there is no public access to the laundry. Nevertheless it remains a memorial to Bath's past industrial heritage.

45. Empire Hotel, Orange Grove/Grand Parade

The Empire Hotel is a large monumental L-shaped block dominating the street corner between Orange Grove and the riverside Grand Parade. The building was designed in 1899 by the architect Charles Edward Davis and in 1907 the wrought- and cast-iron glazed entrance canopies, designed by A. J. Taylor, were added. In 1939, the building was requisitioned by the Admiralty as part of the war effort and was returned to Bath City Council in 1989. The following year the upper floors were converted into apartments and in 1996 the conservatory on the main entrance front was added. The hotel stands five storeys over ground level with corner towers and two further attic floors overhead. Each floor has a string of mullion and transom windows that stretch across the elevations – eight on the main elevation and nine on the riverside. Between the window lines each floor level is marked by a heavy cornice. In addition, the first floor of the main and riverside elevations has an open gallery stretching between the corner towers. Each has four shallow arches carried on columns, with a low-level balustrade between the columns. The roofline of the attic varies between the central double-height Dutch gable and the other plain triangular gables. The upper levels of the pivotal corner tower were given an octagonal layout, with round-headed windows on each face positioned between pairs of columns. Today the ground floor of the hotel is fitted out with bars and restaurants. The upper floors, however, are in residential use and are not accessible to the public.

The main elevation of the Empire Hotel with its floors of mullion and transom windows, variable roof gables and pronounced corner tower.

46. Kingsmead Flats, Green Park Road

Kingsmead Flats is a residential block laid out in a large U-shaped arrangement. This was built by Bath City Council in the 1930s to replace an earlier residential development and was one of the earliest buildings in Bath to dispense with the Georgian and other historic architectural styles and adopt the ideas of the modern movement in architecture. Here, plain undecorated architectural forms were exclusively used and surface ornamentation was eliminated. Each of the four-storey-high blocks had continuous open-access deck along the outer side and open-access staircases to the various levels. In 1992 the development was upgraded by the architects Felden Clegg. This work included closing in the access stairs and eliminating the open decks. Instead, the structure of the decks was adjusted to provide private balconies for the individual flats. At the same time, the ground-level flats were given gardens and an enclosed community landscaped park was created in the inner space of the 'U'. The flats are in private occupation and there is no public access to either the flats or, unfortunately, the communal garden.

Roadside elevation of Kingsmead Flats with recently created private balconies and enclosed access stairs.

The Kingsmead Flats landscaped community park is set into the inner space of the U-shaped block arrangement.

47. New Royal Baths, Beau Street

The New Royal Baths was complete in 2006 and is one of the earliest examples in Bath to depart from traditional Palladian stone-built architectural forms. The building was designed by the architects Donald Insall and Associates and Nicholas Grimshaw and Partners and was successfully slotted into the surrounding historical fabric, partially facing onto Beau Street. The square building is four storeys high and is one of the first buildings in the city to embrace high-tech architecture. This includes a concrete structure faced externally by green-tinted non-load-bearing glazing and narrow geometric framing that, at times, reflects the Bath stone fabric that extends around the site. Elsewhere the hi-tech elements of the building can be glimpsed through gaps in the adjoining street architecture. The internal arrangement has a range of spa and ancillary accommodation on each floor with a circular service tower strategically placed in one corner. The solid upper storey is set back from the main building line and has an open spa pool on the roof.

Glazed elevation and corner tower of the New Royal Baths.

Aerial view of the hi-tech New Royal Baths with rooftop spa. (Permission from Thermae Bath Spa to reproduce this image is gratefully acknowledged)

48. Bath Bus Station, Dorchester Street

The Bath bus station was built on the site of an old electricity building in 2009. The stand-alone building was designed by architects Wilkinson Eyre as part of an overall transport interchange development adjacent to Bath Spa railway station. The site faces onto Dorchester Street with the River Avon immediately behind. The hi-tech building has a simple geometric elegance and consists of a tall elongated

The clear glazing of the Bath bus station waiting area allows passengers clear views of Dorchester Street and the bus stands.

The glass-fronted Dorchester Street elevation of Bath bus station.

single-storey framed structure, which acts largely as the passenger waiting area. This is glazed on all sides and allows passengers to see both into the area and onto the bus parking concourse on the far side, where there are sixteen bus stands. The only traditional enclosed area is the four-storey circular tower at one end that houses the administrative centre and is faced with closely spaced horizontal louvers, beside which is a further small administrative block at right angles to the tower. Despite its small scale the building presents a successful twentieth century architectural image from the railway station, Dorchester Street, Churchill Bridge, and Rossiter Road on the far bank of the Avon River.

A view of Bath bus station corner tower.

49. Holburne Museum of Art Extension, Great Pulteney Street

The Holburne Museum extension was designed by the architects Eric Parry and was completed in 2011. This is positioned at the rear of the eighteenth-century museum and differs significantly in form, character and materials from the original Palladian building. The extension extends over three levels, with each of the upper levels over-sailing the levels immediately underneath. Here the external glazing, green-glazed tiles and fins of the extension break with the material and colour of the original Bath stone building. The ground level is fully glazed, the middle level is partially glazed with the addition of green ceramic vertical fins, while the upper level features solid ceramic tiling and fins. Internally the extension corresponds with the three floor levels of the original building, although the new second level is divided into two sub floors. The ground floor contains the Garden Café while the three upper floors are devoted to display galleries. The café opens onto the attractive garden patio with clear views Sydney Pleasure Gardens beyond.

Left: The form, glazing, tiling and fins of the Holburne Museum extension.

Below: The ground-level Garden Café of the Holburne Museum extension looks out onto the garden patio and Sydney Pleasure Gardens beyond.

50. Roper Building Portal, City of Bath College, St James's Street West

The Roper Building acts as the administrative centre and entrance to the City of Bath College on St James's Street. The college was established in 1957, onto which the Roper Building was added in 2012. The entrance portal on St James's Street is the main entrance of the college and was designed by Stride Treglow architects and represents the most significant aspect of the extension. It is three storeys high and clad in dark coloured zinc that opens directly onto the street. Here the architect's approach was innovative. The entrance consists of a bold rectangular portal with the aperture in an off-centre position. Immediately inside the aperture the glazed entrance screen to the college building is pivoted inwards at an angle from the right-hand corner, so as to provide a wide open gap between the screen and the left face of the portal – an opening that is repeated overhead at roof level. On the far side of the portal an upper-level projecting bay window mirrors the design of the entrance screen and wraps around the corner of the building. In effect the architect has skilfully reworked the idea of the monumental portal form – so common a feature of many public buildings in Bath – in a novel and imaginative fashion that celebrates the relationship between the college and the city community in a decidedly twentieth-century manner.

The dark coloured zinc-clad entrance portal emphasises the entrance to the City of Bath College from the city.

About the Author

Pat Dargan is an architect and planner by profession and lectures in physical planning and design. He has a special interest in the heritage and development of towns and villages and he has published and lectured internationally.

Also by Pat Dargan
Exploring Georgian Dublin, 2008
Exploring Ireland's Historic Towns, 2010
Exploring Irish Castles, 2011
Exploring Celtic Ireland, 2011
Exploring Georgian Limerick, 2012
Georgian Bath, 2012
Georgian London: The West End, 2012
The Georgian Town House, 2013
Edinburgh New Town (co-authored with Carley, Dalziel and Laird) 2015
Dublin in 50 Buildings, 2017
Dublin Pubs, 2018